S0-ALC-541

Poesy in blood: A life in words

By: Art Immured

Poesy in blood: A life in words

Table of Contents

Proem:

Never before would I have believed *I* would be writing the introduction for a book, least of all *my* book; but here I sit, thinking back on a day some fifteen years ago, on a school bus in Fayetteville, Arkansas, when a friend asked to read a few poems I had; and then proceeded to pass them about the bus for all to read... I told myself I would never again write poetry. It wasn't that I was embarrassed, I wasn't; though I've never taken praise well; It was that those words were bits and pieces of me, my heart, my blood, my very *essence*; And I've never been an emotionally open person. I am an introvert and I guard my thoughts, but here were my emotions and thoughts; plucked from my heart and head; passed indiscriminately amongst a group of people who didn't know me... And I don't know that I wanted them to. That day I stopped writing poetry.

Now here I am, more mature — though probably no better a poet — and much has happened to change how I view the world; While I am still that boy that never emoted well; who expressed himself better with Staind and Nine Inch Nails lyrics; who's rational worldview only allowed for the belief in two "deities" greater than himself, Trent Reznor and Maynard James Keenan; Who's brutal honesty got him into more tight situations than a chimney sweep's vocation; I am also different in many ways, one of which being that I am no longer abashed of my past and the horrors that twisted me into the oddity I am today; which has allowed me to take heed of a few people's advice and publish some of my work. While this project is nothing extensive, consider it my introduction; and judging by the reaction to my opuscule, I will decide how to proceed from, or retreat back, into obscurity; Here is to hoping I am well received. *Prost!*

Art Immured, 2016

Intro:

Intro-
A prefix meaning
In; Into; Inward.
In the beginning
Or
At first,
There was me,
quiet —
I never cried much;
So Mom says.
Alone I played —
In the woods;
In my room;
In that sacred
space
behind Dad's recliner;
By the bookshelf,
and the 45 player.
Intro-
spective:
Self-analyzing;
Not drowning in the
sea of silence; But
at home in it;
Comforted by the
quietude.
Thoughts preceding
words;
Ink on paper
rather than
vocal sounds —
Self-expression through

poetic medium.
Intro-
verted:
Alone,
not lonely;
Quality
over quantity —
It's not how loudly,
or how much,
you speak;
But what you
say.
The value of
a word:
'I love you' loses
all meaning when
repeated
too often.
So many ways
to say
what you feel,
if you only
think before you
speak.
Intro-
duction:
Who I am;
Words on paper;
Thoughts and feelings.
Pleased to meet you.

Written on 5.Feb.2016

Bat-Winged Heart:

Don't ask me how it happened,
As I haven't any clue —
I was born to normal parents,
Not some of Eddie Munster's crew —
But over time I noticed that
I wasn't like the Jones';
Black was my favorite color
And I decorated it with bones.
Then of course there was my obsession
With Lily, Elvira, and Morticia —
Perhaps it's that deathly pallor,
But I'll take that over tanned Patricia.
I like listening to Siouxsie and the Banshees,
Type O Negative and The Cure;
Sisters of Mercy, Eurythmics
And Oingo Boingo to be sure.
I love watching Edward Scissorhands,
Rocky Horror and The Crow —
Then of course there is Dark Shadows,
Who doesn't love that show?!
I've only dated Gothic girls,
Not the Hippies or the Preps.
In school my kind weren't invited
To hang out on the schoolhouse steps.
My closest friends were books by Stoker,
Neil Gaiman, Shelley and Brönte;
Look on my shelves and you'll see
Everything from Anne Rice to Dante.
And I'm not the least ashamed —
In fact I'm rather proud
Of my individuality –
I stand out from the crowd!

Goth is part of everything I am —
From my clothing to my art —
And it flows in every drop of blood
Pumped through my bat-winged heart.

Written on 30.Apr.2015

These Arms:

My arms are like a highway map,
Crissed and crossed with lines;
Some were just mere accidents;
Most, I must admit, are mine:
There's a curvaceous blonde in Michigan;
A redhead in Fayetteville;
A night of drunken depression;
And teen angst and bitter pills.
Now and then I look at them,
Some silvery, some wide and white;
And each one re-tells it's story,
Brought from shadows into light:
There's one my father gave me,
Not in hate or rage;
It came from disappointment and love
When they'd released me from a cage.
There's one for my father,
Self-Inflicted in pain of loss;
You can see it aback my right hand —
A morbid, scarred cross.
Some would call me 'cutter,'
And speak of my love affair with a knife;
But they only see the surface,
They know nothing of my life.
How could they know of years long past
And death threats in place of love?
Or divorce, abuse, and hell;
Lost faith in gods above?
I don't expect their understanding;
Nor do I care if they never see
The things that go on inside my mind;
What truly makes me be.

There are two attempted suicides
From stark moments of self-doubt —
But here I stand, a stronger man,
I guess I won those bouts.
A few were caused by animals,
Some by fake and faded friends;
The latter easily forgotten;
The former needn't make amends.
Now here I am, not thirty yet,
Traveling blindly a dead-end road;
But my arms provide me guidance,
While my shoulders bear the load.
I'll never give up fighting this,
My life's worth so much more;
I know because these scars speak volumes
About a life worth living for.
So, when you look upon these arms,
Know few scars have reached the heart;
These lines that mark my body
Do not tear me apart.
Instead they give me strength
And guide me from the dark.
These scars remind me who I am —
And even though broken from my start —
I will always remember what made me
Into a living, breathing piece of Art.

Written on 5.Mar.2013

The Cure:

Beautiful crimson globules trickle down my skin,
The razor slices neatly, as I cut myself again;
Most won't try to understand this, thinking it insane,
And they'll never see how it relieves emotional pain.

The lines that define me have begun to blur;
And, as I bleed, I finally know what it is to be pure.
My life is not so terrible that I can't set it right,
But sometimes this is what I need to make it through the night.

The sanguine stains upon my body excise away my hurt,
While awareness of mortality makes me more alert;
With needle, thread and focus I'll mend myself again;
Having let out all the demons and cleansed myself within.

This rite's not as destructive, as so many often say;
And I'll take it over medicine on any given day;
Let your doctor's prescribe you poisons, that medicate your mind;
I'll have the cure that keeps me lucid, and only scars the rind.

Sneer and call me "Cutter," I'll be that any day;
Because I can face my issues, while you stay doped and rot away.

Written on: 5.Jan.2013

Perseverance:

I was there with you,
In the shadow of the school,
When they laughed and jeered;
When they derided you.
I was there with you ,
When the apples flew;
When they bruised your skin,
They bruised mine too.
I was there with you,
When you felt most alone;
In the box, when dad died,
And you were suicide prone.
I was there with you,
When you felt all was lost,
But wouldn't give up,
No matter the cost.
I'm still here with you now,
As you get to your feet;
Refusing to bow;
Never accepting defeat.
I've looked into your eyes,
And I'm proud to be
Part of what we've become:
This man that I see.

Written on 13.July.2014

SCAR(R)ED:

I don't like this, shine some light into the dark;
Help me understand, just where did this madness start?
Make it stop, it's already left a mark;
Please don't let me go, I'm afraid I'll fall apart.

My childhood torn asunder by a vicious sickness;
And try as I might, there's no way I'll forget this;
But I have to find a way to swallow this thickness,
Else I'll choke to death — Must find a way to prevent this.

There are so many ways to find a happiness in slavery —
A place inside my mind to hide away until a new day breaks;
But facing down inner-demons takes a certain kind of bravery;
And I'm not sure I've got it — Or the kind of strength it takes.

 Now I have to contend with the thing inside that I've become;
Growing up a monster — Unsure if I'm the only one —
And it doesn't help to know, as inside I'm just so numb,
And the secrets that I keep remain with me until I'm gone.

Still, I do not like this; Shine some light into the dark;
Help me understand, just where did this madness start?
Make it stop, I already bear it's mark;
Please don't let me go, I don't want to fall apart.

    Written on 15.May.2013

Bleeding:

Dripping, running, pouring, dropping;
Like rivulets of life spilling out of my veins.
These gorgeous rubies, how they fall;
Down to the tiled floor, where they stain.
Perhaps I cut a little deep this time;
Perhaps not deep enough to ease the pain.
The razor my silent absolver;
Whispering painlessly, keeping me sane.
Odd, the way it flows and flows;
Taking so much without making a sound.
Mystifying, The myriad colors it becomes:
Red to vermillion, now pink, and now brown.
As the water washes it, takes it away,
Hypnotically it swirls 'round.
And when the Black One comes,
Bearing dahlias so white;
He reaches out to me, takes my hand;
Carries me down.

Written on : 28.Oct.2013

Image of a Tortured Youth:

Every day, When I wake and look into the mirror,
I stare into my eyes and see the image of a tortured youth;
I will not cry, nor complain, about what I've been through,
As there's no use, no amount of sympathy could soothe:

I've been down Hell's back alleys, but refuse to be a victim;
Instead I find strength in the wrongs committed by my enemies;
So many things, so many loved ones, have been taken from me,
But I know that they're still with me in his memories.

The beautiful jade-green eyes that shone so brightly as a child
Have grown dull and polluted by two decades of affliction and hate;
Despite trying to mend the damage done throughout these years,
It seems as though the cure has come much too late.

From this bitterness and torment I've become a better man,
Able to accept and cope with all that I've been through;
Though occasionally, I can't deny, I cry for that man
As he sees within himself the tragic image of a tortured youth.

Written on 10.May.2013

Unraveling:

I dip my pen into my veins to write these lines,
Blood-red ink scrawled 'cross the page looks so divine;
Though these words rend me to ribbons with their truth,
I've been reciting them ever since my youth.

Twenty-three years now I've bourne this crushing weight,
And it fills me with unreconciled hate;
The ties that bind have rotted now and fell apart.
Leaving me to haunt this world without a heart.

They say experiencing life's what makes us wise,
But these experiences I've had I don't advise;
I fought through hell to learn from them and become stronger,
Now I don't want to fight this madness any longer.

There are days I wish I could leave this all behind,
To just give in and let the darkness take my mind;
And ironically that torment keeps me sane,
As I write my life in words to ease the pain.

Written on 4.May.2013

Broken Boy:

I wish someone would wake me
From out of this horrid dream;
Can't they hear my cries of torment?
Can't they hear me scream?
My angel left me all alone
After I showed her my worst;
She turned and slowly walked away,
And left me dying here of thirst.
Now I need a place of refuge,
To be sheltered from the storm;
A place so deep within her arms —
As only she can keep me warm.
So I cry, "I am just a broken boy,
Nothing special; Nothing grand;
And as I'll always be a broken boy,
Won't you please just take my hand?
Guide me up and out of here;
Out of my poisoned inner shell.
I will follow you anywhere,
If it will lead me from this hell!"
I've watched molasses hours tick
On the crooked-armed clock;
Thinking of all the time I've spent
On this cold and cursed rock.
I don't know if you can save me
From my self-induced nightmare —
I can't fathom why you'd want to;
Why you'd even really care —
As I am just a broken boy;
Lost and insecure;
Ever just a broken boy
Searching for a cure
 Written on 21.May.2013

A Soul Laid Bare:

Haunted are the eyes of my inner child,
Forced to see too much; Damaged and defiled.
Dancing a stilted tango upon my grave
And mourning the loss of an innocence I couldn't save:

 A purity that was imbrued against my will;
Heinous wounds inflicted, never to heal.
Twisted, tortured, and eviscerated in youth;
Torn apart by fear and unspeakable truths.

Left to battle my demons, alone and afraid;
Abandoned by a god they told me never betrayed.
I've learned a valid lesson retained to this moment:
Blood's no thicker than water, and there's no atonement.

Though we cannot change the past, or the damage done;
One day we must face it, we mustn't always run —
We know this world's not friendly, nor is life fair;
But take this advice from a soul laid bare:

We must take it on ourselves to make things better;
Lest we remain immured in our own fetters.
In the end we become stronger when we face the truth,
And create a sound foundation from our fractured Youth.

Written on 15.May.2013

Sin Eater:

In relative darkness
I hold you tight,
As shadows flicker
In candle light.
The hush consumes us
As you draw the blade
Along your flesh —
Making the pain fade.
No words are necessary,
You know that I'm here,
To kiss your wounds
And chase away your fears.
Bloody lip prints
All along your arm,
To let you know
You'll come to no harm.
We watch the skin part
Before the knife;
Only we know this rite
Takes away your strife.
So darkly beautiful:
The tears on your face;
The smile on your lips;
The way our fingers interlace.
Raising your wrist,
You offer me to drink
Of the blood that stains
Pale flesh like ink;
I press my mouth
To your open skin —
Tasting your darkness;
Taking within me your sin;
Then, caressing your cheek
With my finger tips,

I draw you close
And kiss your lips.
I reach for the candle —
Snuffing the light —
We hold one another
As we're plunged into night.
Here in this darkness
Your absolution is found —
I'm your Sin Eater,
To you always I'm bound.

Written on: 16.Sep.2015

Toy Box Requiem:

' Tick-click-tock' sounds the beat of my damaged heart,

A clockwork figurine – I'm falling apart;

I've been wound-up too often and much too tight,

Now cogs and cranks don't seem to function right.

Like a broken toy soldier relegated to the shelf,

Where there's no one to play with; left to myself;

Can no one see that, though damaged and used,

I'm not fucking worthless, only scarred and abused?

I still have desires and a hunger to live,

If they would just look, they'd see I've so much to give;

And with some time and patience, a friend they could gain,

While for me, I would have someone to help ease my pain.

But instead, here I sit, collecting cobwebs and dust,

As my tears leave fissures of corrosion and rust;

This has become my punishment for believing a lie:

A forgotten animatronic tragedy, left here to die.

Written on:4.May.2013

Sense Me:

Do you hear my words,
When I am speaking from the heart?
Would you really want to know me?
And what makes me fall apart?
Could you feel my pain,
If I shared it with you?
Trace your fingers on my scars?
And help soothe all I've been through?
Can you see my need,
As I open myself to you?
Will you hold me in your arms?
Are my secrets safe with you?
Can you smell my fear,
Without thinking less of me?
Be my candle in the darkness?
Love the rest, not just the best of me?
And will you taste my anger,
On those dark and torrid nights?
Can you care enough to ride the storm?
And still love me when we fight?
Can you use all your senses,
To understand what makes me scream?
Can you look into my eyes ,
And see it's you that makes them gleam?

3.Apr.2013

Bastión

Entre el caos y el vorágine;
Cuando tu vida es oprimida;
No te sientas desamparada;
No seas abatida—
Por que,
En mi, tienes un amigo;
Aqui tienes
Asilo.
Mis brazos puedan ser tu defensa;
Mis manos puedan ser tu espada;
Aqui tienes un castillo,
De ahora hasta la nada—
Por que,
En mi, tienes una fortaleza,
Que nunca
Te abandonara.

15.Aug.2015

November

My favorite season,
I can't give a reason;
It's the fiery golden leaves;
It's the birch and aspen trees;
It's the memories it brings;
It's the many snowy things;
It's November
Remember.
It's the silence of the snow;
It's the fireplace's glow;
It's the icy window panes;
It's the creaking weather vanes;
It's the steaming cup of cider;
It's being snuggled up beside her;
It's November
Remember.
It's realizing that she's gone;
It's the cold and lonesome dawn;
It's a walk amidst the graves;
It's the photos that you saved;
It's her favorite cashmere dress;
It's the remembered last caress;
It's November
Remember.
It's long walks all by yourself;
It's her letters on the shelf;
It's the pink that fills the skies;
It's the tears that sting your eyes;
It's regret for chances not taken;
It's never letting her be forsaken;
It's November
Remember.

It's a single rose upon her stone;
It's the ache of being alone;
It's her name carved in your skin;
It's the sadness and grief within;
It's what keeps her memory alive;
It's for this that we must strive;
It's November
Remember.

16.Oct.2013

In loving memory of Anna Marie Chamberlin
(September 10, 1973 - January 6, 2013)

Fuyu:

The winter comes harsh,
But it's beauty it retains:
Stark; unforgiving.
24.Jan.2015

Hands:

They look like such strong hands,
Capable of many awesome feats:
They can mold, or they can maim;
They can break, or they can create;
They can defend, or they can attack;
They can grasp, or they can let go;
But they just cannot seem to hold.
When I look at them, all I see,
Are empty palms holding empty dreams;
These empty hands aren't what they seem.
They used to hold you; used to enfold you;
Touched, caressed; even spanked and scolded you;
Held your face and wiped your tears;
Protected you from your greatest fears.
But now they're empty; Incomplete;
Unable to fix what I wrought with deceit.
So now I'm alone, watching all my dreams
Sliding away through the cracks and seams;
Unable to hold on, like so much sand;
But they seem like such strong hands.

5.Nov.2013

Kismet:

You were my mirror image,
Despite how you were flawed;
A friend who knew and understood.
Who ever kept me awed.
I thought that I could mend
Your broken heart and mind;
I guess I was a fool to think
There was a cure that I could find.
Lost within your labyrinth;
I tried to guide you through;
But the Minotaur that haunted there
Had finally gotten to you.
There's not a day that passes by
That you aren't in my head;
I don't know how to let you go;
I guess to me you're still not dead.
So every morning when I wake,
I breathe you back to life;
Even though my favorite memories
Often cut me like a knife.
I still sit and write you letters,
On the harder days,
Because there are so many things
I still had left to say.
You're also here, carved upon my flesh;
A living monument to our bond;
The way I let the whole world know,
That you're never truly gone.

Written on 13.Apr.2013
In Loving Memory of Anna Marie Chamberlin
(September 10, 1973 – January 6, 2013)

The Rag Doll and The Skeleton:

A rag doll and a skeleton,
Quite an unlikely pair,
But every bone in his body ached
For rag doll, and this was rare,

They'd stay up all night talking;
As they dreaded being apart;
And the skeleton told the rag doll
That she could have his heart.

"This" the rag doll told him,
"I find a little odd,
For you are but some moldy bones
And a few wilting bits of sod."

So the skeleton led her by the hand
Down through the old cemetery,
To search for the headstone
Where he had once been buried.

There before the enlichened marker,
They found a bush with a single rose;
"It's deepest root" The skeleton told the doll,
"Down to my dead heart goes"

"I wish that you would take this bloom
And with it know you take my heart"
But the rag doll would not pick the flower,
For fear he'd fall apart.

"Thank you for this gift;" She said,
"It means more than you know;
But I would rather leave it,
So your love may ever grow."

Then she took a ribbon that
Was used to stitch her side,
And tied it to the rose that
Lived where he had died.

"To your heart's blood I bind myself
For ever and a day."
The rag doll told the skeleton,
Then took his hand and walked away...

Not two days hence a widowed man
Came to the cemetery to see his wife;
He saw the rose and ribbon there
And cut it with his knife,

Then took and laid it on her grave;
A token of his love:
And knelt to say a whispered prayer
He hoped was heard by god's above

Little did the old man know
The rose he'd cut to take his wife
Was linked to two other lovers
Who'd only just found life...

Rag doll searched for skeleton;
Not knowing where he'd be;
But all she found were his bones
Stretched out under a tree.

There she crumpled, letting her tears
Fall down to wet the gravel,
And held her beloved Skeleton
As she slowly came unraveled.

"I do not understand how this happened,"
The rag doll did softly say,
"The ribbon meant eternity,
Not just one single day."

Then, in one last desperate effort,
She took up all her loose threads
And attached the parti-colored pieces
About her lover's lifeless head...

The old man, upon leaving,
Saw some color amidst the dull,
And on investigating found
A most interesting skull;

Thinking this an odd encounter —
Much like skeletons and rag dolls —
He carried it back down the path,
As he thought it'd lift the pall.

He set the brightly decorated skull
Atop his wife's gravestone
And prayed to Santa Muerte
To not let her feel alone...

Days went by and the rose did wilt
And the ribbon blew away;
But there upon that marble stone
The grinning skull did stay.

Thus it surely can't be said
Rag doll's last effort was in vain;
For she and her dear skeleton
Together for eternity remain.

Written: 28.Apr.2015

Kōryo:

When cherry blossoms
Fall to the earth like snowflakes,
Our pain falls in tears.

24.Jan.2015

Anna's Tree:

"Oh, my big and lonesome tree;
Standing quiet in the wood;
I see you and I feel safe —
As every little girl should.

I look up to your strong branches,
And wish they'd wrap me 'bout;
Lending me their security,
By blocking the world out.

Your canopy protects me from
The sun, the wind and rain;
And when I hold you in my heart,
You protect me from my pain.

Tree, I climb into your limbs;
Where it's dark and cool as night;
And pretend your limbs are human arms,
That quietly wrap me tight.

And if I listen very close,
When the wind is in your leaves,
I think that I can hear your voice —
Whispering to me.

Oh, Tree, Oh, Tree; sad silent tree;
I wish I were the soil,
And you could sink your roots in me —
Depend on me, I'll be loyal.

Oh, Tree, Sometimes I wish you were
A man — the tall and silent kind —

If you were, you'd be my man
And never leave my mind.

Tree, I want the world to know
You're mine, so in your bark
I'll carve my name, for all to see —
As in me you've left your mark.

What sad fate, my silent tree,
That I am just a girl;
And you are but a tall oak tree —
Though to me, you're the world.

I hope one day you come alive —
Free of the prison of the tree —
And no matter, soon or ages,
You come seeking me.

But if this little girl's wishes
Don't come true one day;
Do not rue the days I've waited —
I'd have it no other way.

Tree, Oh, Tree; My lovely tree;
At your roots I'll lay when I die —
So that for eternity
In your embrace I'll lie."

Written on 21.Sep.2015
In Loving Memory of Anna Marie Chamberlin
(September 10, 1973 – January 6, 2013

Yūhi:

When the sun sets and
My present world rests in dark,
The mind sighs; Content.

24.Jan.2015

Elegy for Heathcliff:

In a house, hemmed about by brume,
Presided over by an air of gloom;
Where every mirror is shrouded black
And love is gone — never to come back;
She comes to me, all in matte,
Emerald eyes and a pillbox hat.
Searching from behind her lace veil
To see if I am coping well;
I thank her with a kiss on pallid cheek,
Yet she insists I'm looking peak;
Perhaps it is that smell of clove,
Or her lips of deepest mauve;
But something about her has in me stirred
A desire I had thought interred.
She smiles, as her scent perfumes the air,
Wafting up from the generous, cloven pair;
Satin whispers as she takes the hand,
Where once had been a silver band,
And leads me demurely down the hall;
The staccato of heels echo the pall;
To a room where only candles dance,
She guides me as if in a trance;
Then eases me down to my marriage bed —
The union ended, the bride long dead —▢
Where I watch in wonder, as with a shrug,
Her mourning garb falls to the rug;
Then down she lets her long, dark hair,
And smiles shyly as I stare.
She comes to me where once I slept,
But recently have only wept;
Slow and elegiac, as a dirge,
We embrace; our bodies merge.
Her kiss is soft and bittersweet,
Her body a disquietingly icy treat.
Back lacquered nails dig in my chest
As pearls of sweat drip from her breasts.

I whisper that I love her; and it's no lie:
For this woman I'd surely die.
She assures me I never have to be alone;
Her residence closer than a tossed stone;
And I know I'll see her again and again —
Though our trysts are surely a sin.
At last I fall back into cushions deep
And with a sigh, slip into sleep;
Where I am tormented by her eyes,
Until I'm woken by my own cries.
The room is dark and smells of earth
And of her presence there is a dearth;
I dress, then wander back down the hall
And out to the garden where weeds grow tall.
There before me is a marble stone;
The ground disturbed and nothing sown.
I kneel and trace the graven name,
Wondering at my lack of shame —
She is gone, but my love stays strong,
And still I lust, though it is wrong.
The entire world has become a reminder
That she is never again to bide here —
Must I be as Heathcliff — cursed —
Loving the dead, through best and worst!?
Perhaps her loss has driven me insane,
Hungry to hold what I can't obtain;
I think of last eve and how we laid
Together, as I reach for the spade.

Written on: 11.May.2015

The Awakening

Thirteen stories – One-hundred-and-thirty feet—
Above the city known as London; Dead asleep;
The wind is blowing past two figures there embraced —
Her body to his body, His arms around her waist.
His ebon wings enfold them; A shelter from the storm;
The love that burns between them, all that keeps them warm.
He, a fallen angel; She, a lover of the cursed;
She bends her neck in offering, aware of how he thirsts.
The cathedral stones around them begin to crack and groan
As the gargoyle there below them lets out a chilling moan;
The passion that is extent between the beauty and her beast
Has woken ancient sleepers, that now have a need to feast.
Lost in thoughts of one another, as the creature comes alive,
And flaps its mighty wings — preparing for a dive.
His hands slide lower on her stomach as his lips caress her skin
And her body screams out for his bite — though she knows it is a sin.
For him she'd embrace the darkness and be relegated to the night;
The mistress of a devil, banished forever from the light.
To make her his he'd brave it all, and even face the one God's wrath —
So he whispers that he loves her, then commits them to the path.
As her lifeblood rolls across his tongue; Filling him with delight;
The gargoyle launches from the walls, wings outstretched in flight.
The angel pulls back with a gasp and licks her pale flesh clean,
As she sighs and closes her eyes and back into him leans.
The night is nearly over, though a new life has begun —
One full of love and passion, but cast far from the sun.
They stare into the distance — the awakening complete —
And contemplate existence, as their unified hearts beat;
Standing on a buttress of which a gargoyle was once a part,
Listening to the innocents below, as the screaming starts.
24. Apr.2015

Perspective:

A candle burning in a darkened room,
All about it shadows black as night;
There are those who stand in halo looking out,
Fearing everything hidden from sight;
Then those of us who walk 'midst the umbra,
Choosing this existence to best appreciate the light.

Written 28.Oct.2013

Dark Mother:

Made to be the perfect match
To a spineless, whining fool;
But preferring not to breed poor genes,
She instead chose to be cruel —
So, crying went the wretched Adam,
Begging his god to hear his shouts;
And from the utopian Eden
Poor Lilith was cast out.

For standing proud and demanding respect
She was condemned to exodus;
But in leaving she found Sammael,
And gave life to the rest of us —
Teaching all her children the folly
Of the laws imposed by God;
She raised her young to cherish life,
And love the earth on which they trod.

Unconstrained and undefined are we
By a church's sumptuary laws,
We live, and love, and lust for life:
Making no excuses for our flaws —
Understanding did she give us,
That we're nothing more divine than men;
Driven by our carnal needs,
And knowledge of all seven "sins."

So every day we should raise our glass,
And toast our mother dear;
For giving us a life worth living,
Instead of one spent bowwed in fear;
For imparting us the uncommon sense
To live and love guilt free;
And to see that, had we been in God's image,

Quite pathetic would we be.

Written On 27.July.13

Original Sin:

Perhaps you are one of many who like to believe in Eden;
Though you haven't proof of where it lies, in Africa or Sweden;
Still you cling to the tale of poor, sweet, innocent Adam and Eve;
And the wicked, loving, despotic god who created them without leave.

I'm sure you like to picture the garden, with it's lush and heavenly trees;
To imagine that it's divine beauty could bring you to your knees;
And you probably hate the little serpent, cunning as could be;
Who, with a slick and irreverent tongue, convinced Eve to see.

Maybe you don't like to think the knowledge imparted was a gift;
You probably think it was the very evil that brought about the rift;
That, because of one small bite of fruit, You're stained eternally to the core,
With the knowledge that sweet, little, immaculate Eve was nothing but a whore:

She laid about with serpents, she laid about with men,
She laid about with whomever she chose; Indulging in sin;
Drinking down sweet nectar from Adam's tumescent rod,
She cursed the world to suffer the wrath of a loving god.

And do you ever stop to think about the idiocy of it all?
That if a god really created life, he instilled nature's call?
Thus, did he not give you evil urges and a taste for forbidden fruit?
And did he not then know you'd be doubting and irresolute?

So, If you choose to go one believing, that's all well and good;
But here is something to consider — And for your sake you should —
The original sin never was in the eating of Eve's luscious fruit;
It was when man convinced himself that the eating was the evil's root.

Written on 13.July.2013

The Nature of the Beast:

Have you ever stopped and thought, the old story's told wrong?
That Red Riding Hood wasn't victim, but wolf all along?
How, perhaps, she seduced the woodsman with a promissory look;
Leading him into the forest, where his virtue she took?

Maybe 'feasting on flesh' was quenching her sexual fire,
Fulfilling a need her carnal nature inspired;
Could the eating of granny have had an erotic bent?
And the woodsman have just been a licentious gent?

What if all these years the bards have just been old prudes,
Doctoring the story to fit their moralistic moods?
Twisting the tale in such a way it wouldn't vex;
As originally it spoke of how women too crave sex.

Think for a moment of the color worn by miss red —
Scarlet marked a harlot; A woman skilled in bed.
A thought the old puritans couldn't abide back then —
A sensual woman who embraced earthly sin.

But why frown on a woman for her innate desires?
If it's nature's endowment, who're we to deny her?
Should she choose to be temptress, huntress, or whore,
I'll not begrudge her, nor show her the door.

You can pretend you enjoy playing the idealistic fool;
Or admit we're all born to be Lords of Misrule:
Either way, I choose to indulge myself in life's feast —
For Miss Red and I know, It's the nature of the beast.

Written on 10.Sept.2013

Hope:

Hope,
Like a flickering candle in a sea of black;
Or a helping hand, when you're on your back.
Hope can be a voice on the end of the phone;
Or a letter in the mail that says you aren't alone.
Hope is what keeps us, when all seems lost;
Hope is what we fight for, at all cost.
Hope is what you gave me, when I needed it most;
When I felt defeated; Like giving up the ghost.
So now that I'm here, So far from your reach,
Know I carry that hope — as a torch — Into the breach;
No matter how this goes, your love's brought me light,
To stand 'midst the shadows, not knowing if you're with me in the night.

Written on 4.Jan.2014

Self-Deposition:

I would give it all,
Give up monarchy and crown;
What good are they if still I frown?
Because a king without a queen
Is like a ring without a stone;
A lonely man upon a throne —
Just left to sit there all alone.

No, I would rather be a thrall,
Giving up the hunting and the hounds;
Gladly leave without a sound;
As an emperor sans empress
Is but a groom without a bride;
An empty man with broken pride —
His tear–filled eyes show pain inside.

I'll turn away, I'll leave the hall;
Keep the scepter and the gold;
As without her I'm just so cold.
I'll be a peasant on this path,
As It leads me to my mate;
Call it luck or call it fate —
King no more, but to her still great.

Written on 17.Feb.2014

Unspoken:

You look into my heart
And beg me not to say
What is written there;
But I don't mind —
For I know that love is
A powerful thing,
So much larger than words;
Love need not be spoken,
Love need just be shown —
I can love you as a friend, or
I can love you like no other;
I can love you like a sister, or
I can love you like my lover.
So on this day,
And every day of your life,
Know that I needn't speak a word
To love you,
As a friend, or as my wife.
11.Feb.2014

The Taint:

With nose to wind, I seek
The one thing that can sate
The ache that fills my mind,
My gorgeous moon; My mate.
Paws whisper over many miles;
Eyes vigilant for the prize.
Something faint I taste on the air,
Which causes my hackles to rise;
Slowly, I sniff this newest scent,
Heart racing with unaccustomed fear.
Throwing back my head, I howl; Mournfully;
And from green eyes roll a tear.
Feeling as the dark descends — my moon has been eclipsed
By another; A foreign sun;
Indecision fills my breaking heart —
Do I take back the blighted? Or do I turn and run?
I know it is not possible to continue;
No matter if it's only faint.
With one last, sad breath I turn to go,
No longer able to bear the taint.

Written on 16.Aug.2014

Solitude & Silence:

Silence,
The sound of my heart
No longer beating;
Of life; However fleeting.
The dissonance of those words
That rend me to ribbons
With their sound;
The chaos of losing
Everything I'd found.
The tranquility of never
Again drawing breath;
Of making friends so intimate
With cold and lonesome death.
Never understanding
Why I'd chosen
To let my heart ever
Be unfrozen.
The desire to bring my pain
And aching to an end;
While unable, lest I break
My oath to be here
For you as a friend.
If not for that
I'd drink the Lethe's water
In so deep —
To wash away my sorrow —
To forget why I weep.

Written on 22.Apr.2014

Love:

Love;
Like a rose, or a lily;
With nurturing and care can become
Quite beautiful and fulfilling.
But also, Like a flower;
Sensitive to the cold night;
If handled roughly and unjustly,
Will quickly wilt and die.
16.Aug.2015

The Lethe:

By the banks of the Lethe I sit;
Do I dare to imbibe? Do I dare forget?
When love turns to torment,
We seek release; A cure;
When our hearts turn black,
We see the Lethe's allure.
When the elixir of love
Spoils to a milk of hate;
When Cupid's arrows kill,
Instead of sweetening fate;
The waters so tranquil;
So peaceful; So pure;
The river it calls me —
Promising a fix so sure;
And with one look back
At the image of her face,
I cup my hands and drink deeply;
And get lost in the taste.
05.Apr.2014

BI:

Entre tus ojos
Me encuentro belleza;
Me enamoro.

13.Apr.2015

Daddy:

Anyone can be a father,
The donor of a sperm;
What it takes to be a dad
Is defined by other terms:

A father's hand's may guide you,
Showing you the right path;
But a dad's hands enfold you,
Even in discipline there's no wrath;

A father's voice may scold you,
Correcting you when you stray;
But a dad's voice is full of love,
Even when insisting you obey.

Not every man can be a father;
Nor can every father be a dad;
As every son can't be so lucky
To have the dad I had.

Ten years I've been a father;
And not the best by any means;
But what I strive for is that title
That comes of more than passing genes:

I seek to be the dad
My little girls deserve;
Cherishing and molding those angels
With honor, strength and verve;

So one day they'll look back —
While raising their own kids —

And hope to love their children
The way they know their daddy did.

Written 18.Oct.2014

Longing:

I miss you like I miss
The leaves on autumn trees;
Like a clipper misses wind
When becalmed upon the seas;
I miss you like the murmur
Of a misty rill within a wood;
I miss you like I never,
Ever thought I would.
I miss receiving your letters;
I miss our little talks;
I miss our trading poems;
And I miss our mental walks;
Though I never touched you;
Never even held your hand;
I still look upon your photograph
And wish I was your man.
I miss you and hope you're happy,
Wherever you have gone;
And I wonder if you think of me
In the early morning dawn;
Because not a sunrise rises,
That you aren't in my head;
And not a sunset settles,
That I don't wish you in my bed,
Just so I could wake up to you ;
Feel you right here by my side,
Kiss your lips and tell you
All these things I hide inside.

28.Jul.2014

Temptation:

I hope you're listening,
As I've got something to say;
And I'd like you to hear it
Without delay;
Your eyes drive me crazy;
Your lips drive me mad;
Your curves make me wild;
Your voice makes me bad.
Your hair needs my fingers
Running all through it;
Your skin needs my lips
Acting as our conduit;
Your wrists need pinning
Up over your head,
By my hands as I kiss you,
While we lie in bed.
Your body needs my body;
Your sex needs my love;
Your nails in my shoulders
As I stare down from above.
If you crave it rough,
Or prefer it real slow;
I can fulfill your naughtiest wishes,
I just want you to know:
You're the greatest temptation
This man's had in so long —
And if having you isn't right,
Then I'm fine being wrong.

Written on: 13.Oct.2013

The World Below:

Come with me,
Down the Rabbit Hole —
Into the everlasting
Darkness of the soul.
Come with me,
Down the basement stairs —
Become one of the oddities
That fester there.
This is where
We broken come,
When the norm
Has made us numb;
When we find
There is no love,
For us,
In the world above.
We make the beauties
Our dolls and toys —
Some play with girls;
Some play with boys.
Some like ropes;
And others knives.
Some take innocence;
Or other's lives.
Here are all
Dark secrets kept;
Be you novice,
Or beast adept.
The world above's
Locked safely out —
So no one hears

The screams and shouts.
Seeled eyes;
Stitched–up lips;
Bloody thighs;
Pubescent hips;
We have it all,
 Beneath the floor —
Unlock your mind;
Open the door —
Come downstairs
And you will see
How much fun
The dark can be;
Here you'll find
Acceptance and love —
Things unknown
In the world above.

Written 10.Sep.2015

Last Mile:

I clear the leaves from stones
And read the names;
Nothing left here except bones,
I feel the same.
A heart beats inside skeletal cage,
I want to cry;
A life of sordid sins and rage,
I heave a sigh.
Down lanes and meadows I walk
Toward cemetery gates;
Beside me, as a ghost, my shadow stalks —
Don't know it's fate.
As I pass through creaking bars
I glimpse a rose;
Pushing from the cracks in stone and tar,
It's beauty glows.
Finding this life amidst the dead
I can't but smile;
As I no longer feel the dread
Of the last mile.

Written on 8.Mar.2014

Martyrs:

As devout we worship foreign flesh,
These bodies our temples, our altars so fresh;
We decorate their surface with scars, ink, and steel;
Outward expressions of who we are and how we feel.
But inside we cage the creature that's really us,
Turning from it to embrace self-loathing and disgust;
Pushing down and chaining the thing that makes us great,
Abolishing it as a stigma, only for procreation and hate.
Just to consecrate our lust in the halls of pagan gods,
Casting our dice and playing the odds;
Sacrificing sex with a crown of laurels on our head —
Watching it bleed out and stain our conscience red.
As thieves we taste the ambrosial nectar of iniquity,
Hiding; from the eyes of fellow gods; our victory;
Rather than proudly standing to claim our win,
We hang our heads and ask forgiveness for no sin.
When will we cease to imprison our nature in the dark?
And stop wearing our carnality as a shameful, scarred mark?
Holding high the vital flame that burns within —
Will we ever embrace that beast we are again?

Written on 31.Oct.2013

The Poet:

Stare at the page
Until drops of blood
Appear on your forehead,
Ambrose said;
Filling our lives
With words of the dead;
And what is the purpose,
When we heed not
All our favorite
Aphorisms —
Poetic, is it not?
A life,
Filled with hatred,
Fueled by anger,
Bound by honour.
Ironic?
Or just sad?
An expiring man
Chewing the broken shards
Of life, so unfair;
But of his own creation;
Dying to make
Something of himself;
Only to die
When he makes it.
The bitter agony of defeat;
And poetry just
A way for him to bleed —
Release.
Written on 17.Oct.2014

Walpurgisnacht:

Hear the church bells, how they peal;
Signaling the turning of the wheel;
The sun now sets; Christians to their meals;
While good pagans to the mountain steal.

Out past the forest; Out in the night —
Where most won't tred without fright —
You'll see the flickering bonfire light,
Beckoning the revelers to the rite.

Perhaps black cats creep and bats take wing,
But who takes notice of such mundane things?
We are headed for the feast of spring —
As to the old ways we cling.

No demons, No devils, No sacrifices here —
None of the inanities the ignorant fear —
Only mead horns, food and good cheer —
Of course some witches — and homemade beer!

Tonight we celebrate the ending of the cold;
We celebrate the new calves, kid and foals;
We celebrate the young and growing old —
Kith and Kin and tales yet told.

This night with the old gods we will walk
And drink with friends and joke and talk;
While the Christians tremble behind doors well-locked,
We will be celebrating Walpurgisnacht!

Written on 27.Apr.2015

Wolf Mother:

Her eyes
Pierce the forest;
She searches
For any sign
Of threat —
To her pack;
To her pup.
Her regal head lifts
And she
Howls;
All that hear
Know the sound:
Wolf Mother.
5.Mar.2014

Chamber Music:

I like the ones,
Petite and thin,
With sunny high voices —
My violins;
And I like the ones,
Curvaceous and mellow,
With warm, honeyed voices —
My violoncellos;
No, I don't shun
The full, round waist
And the sonorous voice
Of a stately double bass.
I love them all,
I love to touch their strings;
To embrace their warm bodies;
To make them sing.
Alone in my chamber,
I turn low the light,
Then together we make music
Throughout the night.
A good lover, I listen;
Letting them guide
Where to place my fingers,
To release the warmth inside.
I delay the crescendo —
Be it scherzo, or frantic,
Or a slower adagio —
Profound and romantic.
I know the neighbors listen,
And annoy them I might;
As the music's unending —
From darkness 'til light.
I cannot help my addiction
To these heavenly idols;
These bewitching angels;

These womanly viols.

23.Aug.2015

Breath:

Waiting for your letters
Is like holding my breath;
Like no air's in my lungs
And I'm suffocating to death;
So know that I am here,
Starving to hear I've got mail,
So as to draw one more breath
Before I die in this hell.
28.Jun.2015

Dark Desire

Let me tell you of a dark love —
One I can't disguise —
And in telling know that these lips
Won't ever tell you lies:
I want to stand beside you;
Dry your tears when you cry;
Hold you in my strong embrace;
And make love until you sigh.
I want to guard your closest secrets;
And be your yeanlings sire;
I want to be your darkest fantasy,
Your wolf and your vampire;
To nourish myself from your flesh;
Taste the blood betwixt your thighs;
Explore your deepest darkness,
To understand your hows and whys.
I'll be your guardian Devil;
Walk beside you through the fire;
Protect you from your enemies,
Light your path by their funeral pyres;
I'll show you your true nature;
Animal, woman; sexual, wise;
Teach you to release your inner witch:
Confident wickedness, sensual guise.
I'll love you with my dark passion —
No drug will ever take you higher;
I'll worship your carnal temple,
You'll be the goddess I require;
I'll stare into your soul,
Through the windows of your eyes;
And be your dark desire
Until our very essence dies.   Written on: 1.Dec.2014

Miryō:

The perfume wafts from
Your generous décolletage;
Intoxicating.

28.Jan.2015

Catharsis:

Pink,
The soft blush
Of your skin —
This is only
The beginning.
In truth,
It was a book;
Then questions —
I told you I could;
Had;
That the book was
Not a good window
For which to view
This...
Art form.
But you insisted;
And now?
Pink —
In the rough shape
Of my hand.
A delicate rufescence
On the gentle curvature of
Your bottom,
Soon becomes an angry flush.
Your breath comes
In shallow gasps;
Sweat beads your
Forehead,
And you squirm
On my lap;
Wrists bound;
Knuckles white;

Eyes closed;
Expensive lace...
Saturated.
Gentle caresses
Between
Firm swats,
Cause frissons
Of desire —
Confusion —
You babble,
"Sorrys," "Nos," "Pleases;"
But
Never *the* word.
You beg; You pout; You...
Cry.
To think,
That a book —
A whim —
Led to this;
To such
Catharsis.

Written on: 27.Nov.15

Yūwaku:

Your full lips glisten
And seduction drips lewdly —
I am tantalized.

28.Jan.15

Aberrant Fetish:

I know they say
It's taboo,
But I cannot
Help
This
Infatuation;
This
Desire —
The urge to reach out;
To caress;
To kiss your
Smooth,
White flesh.
I can picture us,
In my mind's eye:
You astraddle me
In the dark;
Your head thrown back,
Lips forming a sensuous
"O";
My lips on your neck;
Sweat
Beading our skin as
You caress my head;
My fingers grip your
Luscious bottom,
And you
Envelope me...
Completely.
Your hands try
To guide
My lips to your

Breasts;
To a lewdly erect
Nipple.
Why is this
A Sin?
This
Wholly consensual;
Wholly beautiful;
Wholly flawless
Congress we hold
In my bed.
I do not know where I end,
And where you begin.
One heart beat;
One breath;
One...

I press you back
Into
The pillows;
My hands become
Fleshly manacles
About your wrists,
And I
Kiss
Your exquisite
Mouth.
Tongues
Dance;
Breath
Shared.
We moan
As one.
You bite my lip
And I shudder.

Sitting back to
Admire you —
Pinned —
Like a voluptuous
Butterfly —
By my love —
To the bed.
You smile;
Oh, so seductively;
And pull me back
Down,
Into your arms;
Into
Heaven —
The only heaven
I believe in.
You moan
My name,
And I know:
Aberrant;
Sinful;
Wrong;
This is none of
Those things;
This is:
Our secret;
Our heaven;
Our forbidden
Sip
Of 1922
Whiskey —
Prohibition be damned!
Your fingers
Grip
Black satin

Sheets;
Your back arches;
Breasts thrust out;
We merge —
Your liquid heat
Coats —
Vesuvius!
My liquid heat
gushes —
Geysir!
And we collapse;
Panting;
Connected;
One...

My mind's eye
Closes.
I spill
Decadent pearls
Of iniquity
In violent splashes of lust
Onto the sheets,
And breathlessly
Contemplate this —
This...
Aberrant Fetish.

Written on: 19.Sep.2015

Ikken:

Your skirt rides up and
Reveals creamy, stockinged thigh —
Exquisite; Taboo.

28.Jan.2015

Masterpiece:

This is how I love you:
Wrists bound to the headboard,
Exquisite, alabaster skin
Laid out before me —
Like a blank canvas.
In the flickering candle light,
Your breasts rise,
Erotically,
With every breath.
Blindfolded,
You do not see
The black rose in my right hand,
Nor
The quill pen in my left.
I savor the moment;
The beads of sweat;
The frisson;
The way your areolae
Grow taut
As the rose petals trace
Your sumptuous curves —
You moan,
Softly.
I am a poet.
And you?
You are my canvas —
Every
Delicious
Inch of you.
Dipping the nib,
Delicately,
Into your moist well;
I begin:

I write —
Prose;
Odes;
Laudations;
Haiku —
With your essence,
Across your flesh.
Is this a sin?
If this is sin,
You are my bible.
I scroll invisible words
Along your neck;
Over your breasts;
Down your thighs;
And if I err,
I slowly erase the word
With gentle strokes
Of my tongue.
Your nectar drips –
Beautifully.
Your petals blooming
With every
Dip
Of my pen.
You squirm;
Writhing;
Sinuously;
As I lay the rose
Between
Your generous breasts,
And sign this —
My poetic masterpiece —
"Mine."
Written on 2.JUL.2015

Unbowwed:

An oddity
From start to finish;
Call me what you will,
But it won't diminish
Who I am inside;
What I've become —
Or the fact that you hate,
And you are so numb;
Or the fact that I have,
Where you have none.
So that's it, it's over
And we are done;
So turn away, but don't walk,
Feel obliged to run;
I'm not going to change
For you or your friends,
I refuse to feel shame
When time comes to an end;
No, I won't look back
To find my life was wasted,
I'll be proud to have lived,
Knowing each drop was tasted.
Sure, I've done some wrong,
But I live and learn;
My mistakes don't break me —
They're lessons earned.
I've no bones in my closet,
Just an empty grave —
My secrets aren't my master,
Nor am I their slave.
What difference does it make
If my youth was rough?

That's no excuse to play the victim,
Hell, it made me tough —
At night when I slept
And demons sang me songs,
I never let them scare me –
I sang along.
I faced down each opponent,
Fear, and fake friend;
And not a single one brought me
And an end.
So why would you think
I'd fall at your feet now?
Or change my wicked ways?
That, like you, I'd bow
To the will of a lord
And unloving master,
Who's only accomplishments
Are to bring disaster;
And make you forsake
This life and crave death?
Who forgives the ones
Who rapes kids and smoke meth;
If you ask me —
And I know that you won't —
You're a poster child
For everything that I don't
Ever want to be,
And I'll say it aloud:
I'm a sinner, friend;
This head is unbowwed.

12.Apr.2016